SERIES TITLES

PREHISTORY **I**

MESOPOTAMIA AND THE BIBLE LANDS **II**

ANCIENT EGYPT AND GREECE **III**

THE ROMAN WORLD **IV**

ASIAN CIVILIZATIONS **V**

AMERICAS AND THE PACIFIC **VI**

EARLY MEDIEVAL TIMES **VII**

BEYOND EUROPE **VIII**

LATE MEDIEVAL EUROPE **IX**

RENAISSANCE EUROPE **X**

VOYAGES OF DISCOVERY **XI**

BIRTH OF MODERN NATIONS **XII**

XIII SETTLING THE AMERICAS

XIV ASIAN AND AFRICAN EMPIRES

XV THE INDUSTRIAL REVOLUTION

XVI ENLIGHTENMENT AND REVOLUTION

XVII NATIONALISM AND THE ROMANTIC MOVEMENT

XVIII THE AGE OF EMPIRE

XIX NORTH AMERICA: EXPANSION, CIVIL WAR, AND EMERGENCE

XX TURN OF THE CENTURY AND THE GREAT WAR

XXI VERSAILLES TO WORLD WAR II

XXII 1945 TO THE COLD WAR

XXIII 1991 TO THE 21ST CENTURY

XXIV ISSUES TODAY

This Zak Books edition was printed in 2009. Zak Books is an imprint of McRae Books.

VOYAGES OF DISCOVERY

was created and produced by McRae Books Srl
Via del Salviatino, 1 — 50016 — Fiesole (Florence), (Italy)
info@mcraebooks.com
www.mcraebooks.com

Publishers: Anne McRae, Marco Nardi
Series Editor: Anne McRae
Author: Neil Morris
Main Illustrations: Giorgio Bacchin p. 42; Lorenzo Cecchi pp. 18–19; Francesca D'Ottavi p. 21; Emmanuelle Etienne p. 41; Valeria Feretti p. 29; Giacinto Gaudenzi pp. 26–27, 30–31;
Alessandro Menchi p. 13; Antonella Pastorelli pp. 14–15, 33; Claudia Saraceni pp. 16–17; Sergio pp. 24–25, 38–39
Illustrations: Studio Stalio (Alessandro Cantucci, Fabiano Fabbrucci)
Maps: M. Paola Baldanzi
Photos: Bridgeman Art Library, London/Alinari Photo Library, Florence pp. 10–11b; 22–23, 35b; © Stapleton Collection/Corbis pp. 44–45c; Fujita Museum of Art, Osaka p. 6–7b; Photo RMN / © Daneila Arnaudet pp. 36–37; Scala Archives, Florence pp. 9b
Art Director: Marco Nardi
Project Editor: Loredana Agosta
Layouts: Starry Dog Books Ltd.
Research: Loredana Agost
Editing: Tall Tree Ltd, London
Repro: Litocolor, Florence

Consultant:
Dr. Ronald Fritze is a historian of early modern Europe and England. He is the author of New Worlds: The Great Voyages of OF Discovery (Sutton/Praeger, 2003). He appeared on the History Channel series The Conquest of America and is a member of the Society for the History of Discoveries. Currently he is beginning work on a brief biography of Christopher Columbus.

Library of Congress Cataloging-in-Publication Data

Morris, Neil, 1946-
   Voyages of discovery / Neil Morris.
        p. cm. -- (History of the world)
   Includes index.
   Summary: "A detailed overview of the history of the age of exploration, including explorers from all parts of the world and how they brought knowledge of distant lands back to their people, between 1150 and 1750"--Provided by publisher.
   ISBN 978-8860981547
   1. Discoveries in geography--History--Juvenile literature. 2. Explorers--History--Juvenile literature. I. Title.
   G175.M68 2009
   910.9--dc22
                                        2008008409

Printed and bound in Malaysia.

HISTORY

Voyages of Discovery

Neil Morris

Consultant: Ronald H. Fritze, Dean of
Arts and Sciences and Professor of
History, Athens State University, Alabama

Zak
BOOKS

Contents

5 Introduction

6 Spirit of Adventure

8 Mapmaking
   and Geography

10 East Meets West

12 Chinese Exploration

14 Europeans in Asia

16 The Spice Trade

18 Seafaring Vessels

20 Ocean Voyages

22 African Exploration

24 The Slave Trade

26 The Voyages of Columbus

28 Around the World

30 A Spanish Empire

32 South America

34 New Discoveries

36 Missionary Work

38 Rediscovering North
   America

40 Early North American
   Exploration

42 The Arctic Region

44 Australasia and the Pacific

46 Glossary

47 Index

This map showing the east coast of Africa and India was created by Portuguese mapmaker Diego Homem (active mid-16th century) in 1558.

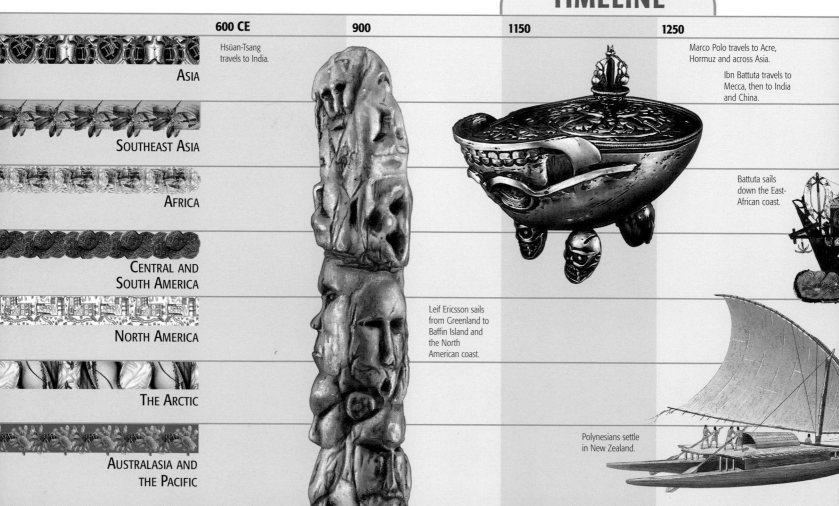

TIMELINE

	600 CE	900	1150	1250
ASIA	Hsüan-Tsang travels to India.		Marco Polo travels to Acre, Hormuz and across Asia.	Ibn Battuta travels to Mecca, then to India and China.
SOUTHEAST ASIA				
AFRICA				Battuta sails down the East-African coast.
CENTRAL AND SOUTH AMERICA				
NORTH AMERICA		Leif Ericsson sails from Greenland to Baffin Island and the North American coast.		
THE ARCTIC				
AUSTRALASIA AND THE PACIFIC			Polynesians settle in New Zealand.	

4

Introduction

People began making long journeys of discovery in ancient times. Many of these were on foot, but increasingly explorers took to ships in a bold attempt to discover as much as they could about their world. This led to a great European "Age of Discovery," as maritime nations searching for wealth and new lands to conquer sent explorers to find a sea route to Asia. Navigators were not always sure where their voyages led them: Columbus thought he had found the Indies, until others realized that he had sailed to a "New World." Later explorers went in search of unknown southern continents and mythical kingdoms filled with gold. This book tells the story of the exciting voyages of discovery that took place over many centuries.

This Aztec drawing shows Spanish conquistadors on horseback and their Mexican allies attacking the Aztecs at Cholula, Mexico.

The great Portuguese explorer Alfonso d'Albuquerque (c. 1453–1515) claimed Goa, The Spice Islands and Ceylon (present-day Sri Lanka) for the crown of Portugal.

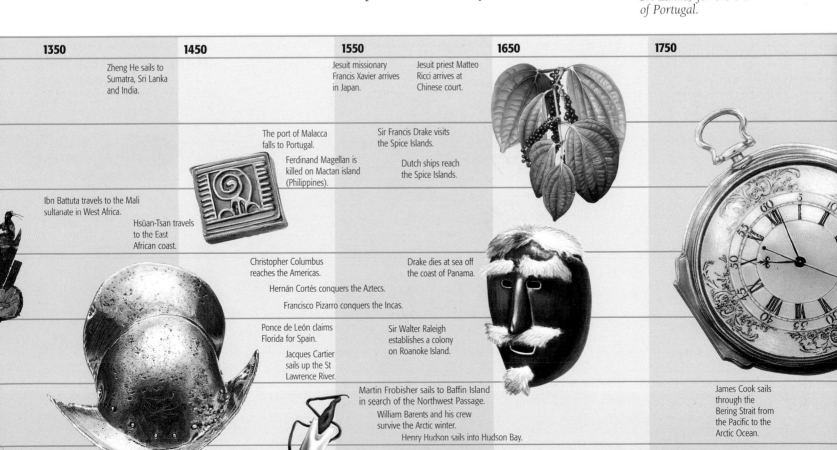

1350	1450	1550	1650	1750

Zheng He sails to Sumatra, Sri Lanka and India.

Jesuit missionary Francis Xavier arrives in Japan.

Jesuit priest Matteo Ricci arrives at Chinese court.

The port of Malacca falls to Portugal.

Sir Francis Drake visits the Spice Islands.

Ferdinand Magellan is killed on Mactan island (Philippines).

Dutch ships reach the Spice Islands.

Ibn Battuta travels to the Mali sultanate in West Africa.

Hsüan-Tsan travels to the East African coast.

Christopher Columbus reaches the Americas.

Drake dies at sea off the coast of Panama.

Hernán Cortés conquers the Aztecs.

Francisco Pizarro conquers the Incas.

Ponce de León claims Florida for Spain.

Sir Walter Raleigh establishes a colony on Roanoke Island.

Jacques Cartier sails up the St Lawrence River.

Martin Frobisher sails to Baffin Island in search of the Northwest Passage.

James Cook sails through the Bering Strait from the Pacific to the Arctic Ocean.

William Barents and his crew survive the Arctic winter.

Henry Hudson sails into Hudson Bay.

Alvaro de Mendaña reaches the Solomon Islands.

Dutch explorer Jacob Roggeveen is the first European to see Easter Island.

Louis-Antoine de Bougainville visits the Solomon Islands.

Abel Tasman reaches the island of Van Diemen's Land (modern Tasmania).

Cook claims the east coast of Australia for Britain.

Spirit of Adventure

People traveled and explored long before the great age of European discovery. Ancient explorers included the Egyptians and Phoenicians. The ancient Greeks looked for new lands to conquer and colonize, and made notes of what they found on their journeys. The Romans and Chinese were also great travelers, and they opened trade routes across land and sea. These early journeys helped expand knowledge of peoples and cultures around the world.

This plate from Mongol-ruled Persia is decorated with a camel caravan.

The Silk Route

Camels carried silk, spices, and other expensive goods from the East along the Silk Road—a series of tracks across the deserts and mountains, leading to Central Asia and beyond. The Silk Road was the main artery of Asian land exploration before 1500, and oasis towns grew up along the route.

Camel caravans were the safest means of crossing desert regions.

This 2nd-century CE painted glass vase was found at Begram, in present-day Afghanistan. It came from Alexandria, in Egypt.

Long Journeys

Many early journeys were long and difficult, especially in rugged regions. Camels were used to cross the great deserts of the world. They helped traders carry spices from southern Arabia to the Mediterranean. In the early 5th century, Chinese travelers walked across the deserts of Central Asia all the way to India. They sailed back to China across the Indian Ocean via Sumatra, making a round trip of at least 9,500 miles (15,000 km).

This 11th-century North American antler wand shows faces that may represent European Vikings.

Spreading Culture

The Chinese Buddhist monk and traveler Hsüan-Tsang (c. 602–664 CE) left the Tang capital of Chang-an in 629 for the long journey to India. On his way he was given a group of packhorses by the king of Turfan, and he walked and rode to southern India and back. As well as learning Sanskrit and studying and translating Buddhist texts, Hsüan-Tsang gathered information about the history and geography of the lands he visited. He may also have helped spread the cultural traditions of Tang China.

Early Voyages

Both the Polynesians and the Vikings were skilled boat-builders and navigators. These skills allowed them to go on long voyages in search of new land. The Polynesians sailed across the Pacific from Southeast Asia in their ocean-going canoes. They colonized Samoa, Tonga and eventually New Zealand. At the beginning of the 11th century, Vikings crossed the Atlantic Ocean from Norway to North America via Iceland and Greenland. They set foot on American soil nearly 500 years before Christopher Columbus.

A Polynesian double-hulled canoe with a triangular sail made of coconut fiber or plaited leaves.

Hsuan-Tsang arrives back in Chang-an laden with manuscripts and precious objects. He was received by the Chinese emperor, although he had never been granted permission to leave the Tang Empire.

EARLY EXPLORATION

399–412 CE
Chinese Buddhist monk Fa Hsien (c. 337–442) walks to India and sails back.

629–645
Hsüan-Tsang travels to India.

c. 800
Vikings sail to the Scottish and Faeroe Islands.

c. 985
Norwegian Viking Eric the Red (c. 950–1003) sails from Iceland to Greenland and colonizes it.

c. 1002
Eric's son Leif Ericsson (c. 980–1020) is the first European known to have discovered North America.

c. 1100–1165
Life of the Moroccan Muslim geographer al-Idrisi.

c. 1200
Polynesians settle in New Zealand.

Mapmaking and Geography

The first mapmaking work of the Middle Ages was undertaken by Muslim scientists in the 9th century. They translated into Arabic the important writings of the Greek geographer, Ptolemy (c. 100–165 CE). In Europe, early Medieval maps were symbolic rather than realistic. By the 13th century, geographers were also producing portolan maps, which acted as navigation charts for sailors. Maps, sea charts, and greater geographical knowledge all helped travel and exploration.

A stick chart from the Marshall Islands of the Pacific. The shells represent islands, and the palmleaf ribs show wave swells and currents.

Chinese Geography

Mapmakers were at work in China at the same time as Ptolemy. By the 12th century CE, Chinese geographers were carving maps in stone, including features such as coastlines and rivers. In 1155, the world's first printed map was also produced in the Song Empire of China. Most Chinese maps were based on a grid of rectangles or squares.

Ancient Knowledge

Following in the tradition of the Babylonians and the Egyptians, the ancient Greeks made advances in surveying and geography. In around 200 BCE, Eratosthenes (c. 276–194 BCE) calculated the Earth's circumference with astonishing accuracy. He was followed at Alexandria by the great astronomer Ptolemy, who wrote an eight-volume *Guide to Geography*. This included maps of the then known world—the continents of Europe, Africa, and Asia.

A 15th-century Flemish portrait of Ptolemy.

Diagrammatic Charts

From the 7th century onward, Christian monks drew the world in a symbolic diagram. They made so-called T–O maps, which divided the world (by a T) into the three known continents and surrounded them with a great ocean (shaped like an O). They included the four compass directions. Christians believed that the T also represented the cross, and that Jerusalem lay at the very center of the map.

The Don and Nile rivers form the top of the T.

Below: This T-O map was printed in 1472.

The Mediterranean Sea divides Europe from Africa.

Great ocean surrounding the world.

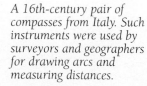

A 16th-century pair of compasses from Italy. Such instruments were used by surveyors and geographers for drawing arcs and measuring distances.

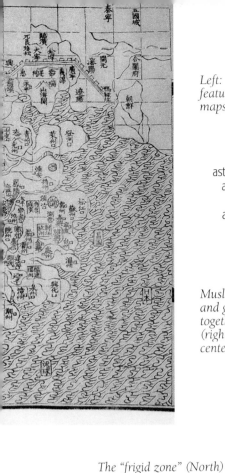

Left: This 16th-century map of China, featuring the Great Wall, was based on maps made more than 200 years earlier.

The World of Islam

The early Muslims were expert astronomers, and learnt a great deal about the Earth. The famous 12th-century Moroccan geographer al-Idrisi had traveled widely by the time he was asked by Roger II of Sicily (reigned 1093–1154) to produce a map of the world.

Muslim astronomers, astrologers, and geographers worked together in observatories (right), which were great centers of learning.

East was traditionally shown at the top.

The "frigid zone" (North) is to the left

This Venetian mappa mundi was produced in 1442. The Easter calendar and zodiac encircle the map.

Mappae mundi

From the 13th century, Christian geographers created more realistic maps known as *mappae mundi* (literally "sheets of the world"). Our word "map" comes from these charts, which were generally produced on sheets of vellum. A *mappa mundi* kept to the basic T–O model, but without formal divisions. Some of the maps may have been used as route plans for traveling pilgrims.

The "torrid zone" (South) is to the right.

East Meets West

Between the 13th and 15th centuries, Christian and Muslim travelers ventured to the Far East. This brought them into contact with the Mongols, both at their capital of Karakorum and later in Yuan-Dynasty China. Accounts of these journeys allowed many Westerners to learn about Eastern ways for the first time. The two greatest travelers were Marco Polo (c. 1254–1324) from Venice and Ibn Battuta (c. 1304–1377) from Tangier. Both made important contributions to geographical knowledge.

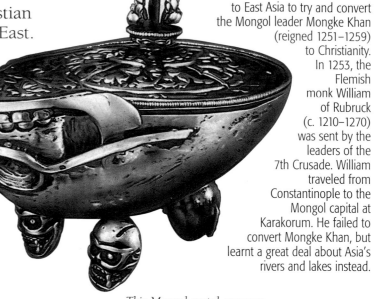

An Arab dhow, which was traditionally used to sail the Indian Ocean.

During the Crusades

Several Franciscan friars traveled to East Asia to try and convert the Mongol leader Mongke Khan (reigned 1251–1259) to Christianity. In 1253, the Flemish monk William of Rubruck (c. 1210–1270) was sent by the leaders of the 7th Crusade. William traveled from Constantinople to the Mongol capital at Karakorum. He failed to convert Mongke Khan, but learnt a great deal about Asia's rivers and lakes instead.

This Mongol metal cup was fashioned in the shape of a skull. It was used as a ceremonial object.

Muslim Exploration

The 12th-century Moroccan geographer al-Idrisi traveled through much of Europe and Southwest Asia 200 years before Ibn Battuta. Having produced a world map for the Norman king of Sicily, Roger II, al-Idrisi wrote a geographical guide book that was also based on reports from other travelers.

A 15th-century painting of Marco Polo and his father Niccolò kneeling before Khubilai Khan.

EARLY VOYAGES OF DISCOVERY

EUROPE
TANGIER
VENICE
ASIA
CONSTANTINOPLE
AFRICA
KARAKORUM
ACRE

→ Polo 1260–1269
→ Polo 1271–1295
→ Battuta 1325–1327
→ Battuta 1328–1330
→ Battuta 1330–1346
→ Battuta 1349–1354

MECCA
HORMUZ
DELHI
CHUAN-CHOU
ARABIAN SEA
CALICUT
INDIAN OCEAN

The Journeys of Marco Polo and Ibn Battuta

Both travelers made long overland journeys and coastal voyages, covering much of the same territory. During his stay in China, Marco Polo traveled to the south of the country, before sailing by junk from the port of Chuan-chou. He was accompanied at the Khan's request by a Mongol princess, who traveled to Persia to become a chieftain's bride. Battuta's voyages also took him along the coasts of China, as well as those of India and Africa.

Marco Polo and the Khan

Marco Polo was introduced to Asian travel at a young age. His father and uncle had already journeyed to the Far East when they invited 17-year-old Marco to join them on a visit to China (then called Cathay). They traveled much of the way by camel. Khubilai Khan, Mongol ruler of the Yuan Dynasty in China (reigned 1260–1271), welcomed them at his summer palace. When Marco Polo finally arrived back in Venice, in 1295, he wrote a book about his travels.

Ibn Battuta

The Arab traveler Ibn Battuta was born in Tangier (in present-day Morocco). His travels began with an Islamic pilgrimage to Mecca at the age of 21, and continued for another 24 years. He recorded his journeys, which covered more than 74,000 miles (120,000 km), in a book named *Rihlah* (Travels). His voyages took him all around the coast of Asia and to Northwest Africa.

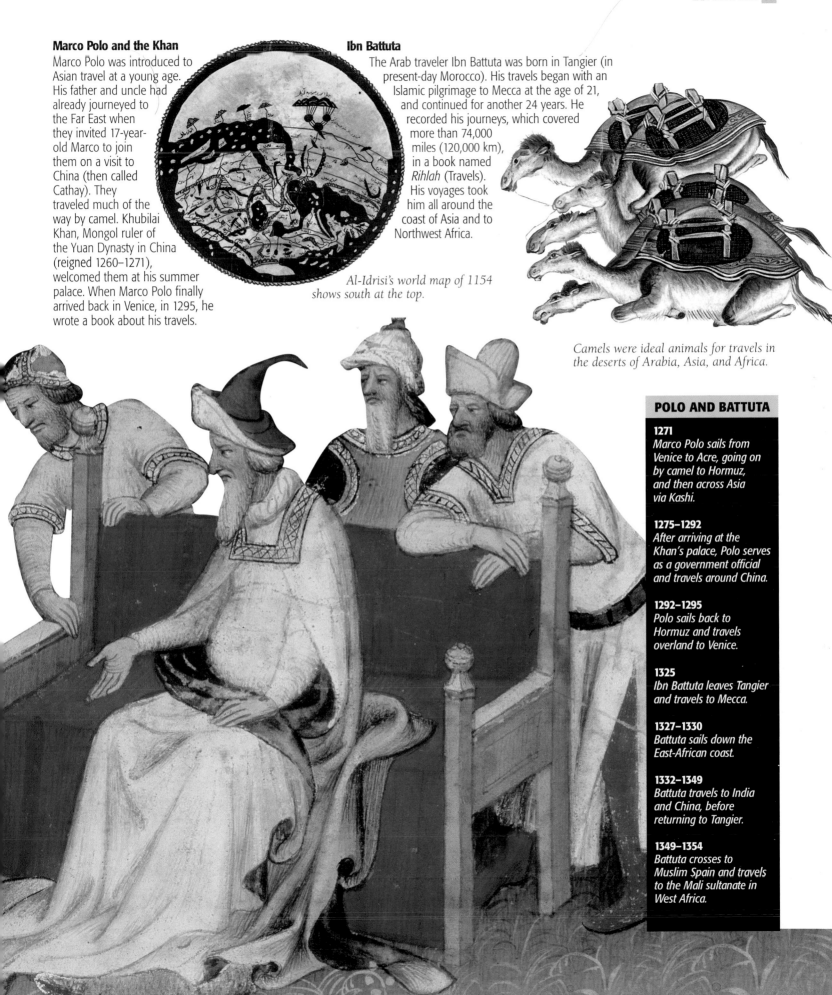

Al-Idrisi's world map of 1154 shows south at the top.

Camels were ideal animals for travels in the deserts of Arabia, Asia, and Africa.

POLO AND BATTUTA

1271
Marco Polo sails from Venice to Acre, going on by camel to Hormuz, and then across Asia via Kashi.

1275–1292
After arriving at the Khan's palace, Polo serves as a government official and travels around China.

1292–1295
Polo sails back to Hormuz and travels overland to Venice.

1325
Ibn Battuta leaves Tangier and travels to Mecca.

1327–1330
Battuta sails down the East-African coast.

1332–1349
Battuta travels to India and China, before returning to Tangier.

1349–1354
Battuta crosses to Muslim Spain and travels to the Mali sultanate in West Africa.

Chinese Exploration

Early in the Ming period of imperial rule, at the beginning of the 15th century, the Chinese undertook a number of remarkable voyages. They were led by a commander named Zheng He (c. 1371–1435), who sailed from eastern China to the Indian Ocean seven times. He reached the coast of East Africa, and it has been suggested that he might have sailed even further. The voyages spread Chinese influence and gathered wealth and trading contacts.

Zheng He brought a giraffe from Africa as a gift for the emperor.

Zheng He's Early Life

Zheng He was born into a Muslim family in the southern Chinese province of Yunnan, which was then controlled by the Mongols. He was the son of a rural official. In 1382, when Ming invaders overthrew the Mongols, Zheng was captured, ritually castrated, and sent to work in the army. In 1390, he was moved to the court of a Ming prince, Zhu Di, who would later become emperor. Zheng was a successful junior officer and was chosen to command the Chinese fleet.

ZHENG HE'S VOYAGES

1405–1407
Zheng He sails with 317 ships and nearly 28,000 men to Sumatra, Sri Lanka and India.

1407–1409
Returns foreign ambassadors who had been collected on the first voyage to Sumatra and India.

1409–1411
To India; involved in civil war in Sri Lanka and wins battle.

1413–1415
To the Arabian Sea and the Persian Gulf port of Hormuz.

1417–1419
To the southern Arabian Peninsula and East African coast (Somalia and Kenya).

1421–1422
To East Africa, returning foreign ambassadors.

1431–1433
To the Red Sea, Mecca, and the Swahili coast of East Africa.

Decorated porcelain was the best-known product of the Ming period. The vase shows the famous Ming design.

Ming China

The first Ming Dynasty emperor came to power in 1368. Under Ming rule, agriculture improved and peasants were encouraged to own land. An early period of expansion included the great voyages around the Indian Ocean. But China's seafaring ambitions died with Zheng He, as the emperors lost interest and became more inward-looking. Nevertheless, the Ming period remained very important in the arts.

Right: Zheng He's fleet used a magnetic compass like this one for navigation.

The Chinese Fleet

The largest vessels in the fleet, including the commander's flagship, were "treasure ships". These were nine-masted giants, up to 72 feet (122 m) long and 170 feet (52 m) wide, and there were about 60 of them. They were the largest wooden ships ever built. They were supported by five-masted supply ships, troop transports, and smaller vessels, making a total fleet of more than 300 ships.

For size comparison, a Chinese treasure ship dwarfs a 15th-century European ship (as sailed by Columbus and Vasco da Gama).

Zheng He commands his fleet from aboard his flagship.

CHINESE EXPLORATION

→ Zheng He's route 1431–1433

→ Other ships of Zheng He's expedition

MECCA
HORMUZ
SUZHOU
AFRICA
ASIA
ARABIAN SEA
CHITTAGONG
MALINDI
CALICUT
INDIAN OCEAN
MALACCA
SURABAYA

Zheng He's Voyages

Zheng He explored the Indian Ocean, which the Chinese called Xi Yang (the Western Ocean). All seven voyages began from the port of Nanjing and the mouth of the Chang Jiang. The fleet sailed through the Straits of Malacca to the Indian Ocean, heading northwest for India and, later, the Arabian Sea and East Africa. It has been suggested that they carried on to the Atlantic and the Americas, but there is little evidence for this.

Europeans in Asia

In the 1480s, Portuguese explorers attempted to reach India by two routes. The first was via the Mediterranean, Africa, and Arabia, and the second was a sea route around Africa. Both attempts were soon successful. Pero de Covilhão arrived in India from the east coast of Africa in 1489. Nine years later, Vasco da Gama became the first European to reach India entirely by sea when he led four ships into the port of Calicut.

A 16th-century illustration of the busy port of Calicut.

A Portuguese colonist is transported in style by her Indian servants.

The Portuguese in India

In 1503, Alfonso de Albuquerque (c. 1453–1515) followed da Gama's route to India and built a fort at Cochin, south of Calicut. This laid the foundation for Portugal's Asian empire, and Albuquerque became governor in 1509. The following year, he captured Goa from its Muslim rulers, and the colony was to remain Portuguese for over 450 years. Missionaries and settlers established the Roman Catholic Church in Goa, and 16th-century colonial buildings still stand there.

Portuguese glazed earthenware bowl with the motif of a carrack (merchant ship).

Golden Goa

When he captured Goa, Albuquerque planned to use it as a naval base against Muslim traders. It also became a useful port for Portuguese trade, especially for spices from Southeast Asia. Gold and other valuables were traded, and the colony became known as "Golden Goa." The Hindu rulers accepted the Portuguese colonies in India, and Goa became the capital of their eastern empire.

Across the Indian Ocean

The map shows the routes taken to India by Pero de Covilhão (c. 1450–1526), Vasco da Gama, Alfonso de Albuquerque, and Francisco de Almeida (c. 1450–1510), the first viceroy of Portuguese India. After rounding the Cape of Good Hope, sailors stopped at Portuguese trading posts on the east coast of Africa before crossing to India.

PORTUGUESE EXPLORERS

LISBON
EUROPE
AFRICA
ATLANTIC OCEAN
ASIA
MOGADISHU
MALINDI
KILWA
COCHIN
GOA
CALICUT
CAPE OF GOOD HOPE
INDIAN OCEAN

→ de Covilhão 1487–1489
→ Da Gama 1497–1499
→ Almeida 1505–1509
→ Albuquerque 1507–1511

East Indian natives row out to greet the Portuguese ships.

Vasco da Gama presents himself to the Zamorin, the Hindu ruler of Calicut, with a letter from the King of Portugal.

Vasco de Gama

Vasco da Gama (c. 1460–1524) was a great sea captain and explorer. He completed his first voyage from Lisbon to Calicut with four ships and a crew of about 170 men. However, the poor selection of gifts he carried with him did not go down well with the Hindu ruler of Calicut, and da Gama stayed for only three months. He made two further voyages to India, and in the year of his death was appointed Portuguese viceroy of the Indian colonies.

A wooden statue of an archangel from one of da Gama's ships.

Fight for Control

Javanese and Chinese merchants had traded spices with India for many centuries before the Europeans. The Indian trade was run by Muslim merchants, who also sailed to Southeast Asia, and in Europe it was run by the Venetians. The situation changed when the Portuguese discovered the sea route from Lisbon to the Spice Islands in the early 16th century. They were soon followed by the Dutch and British.

A British merchant is tortured by the Dutch in the East Indies.

The Spice Trade

The spice trade was very important in ancient and Medieval times. Spices were highly valued in Europe for preserving and flavoring food, especially meat that had been kept in salt. European explorers were sent to find the original source of these wonderful goods, which were usually traded by Muslim Arabs acting as middlemen. There was great competition between the maritime nations, as they fought to discover and then control the world's spice routes.

SPICES

1511
The Muslim port of Malacca, on the Malaysian coast, falls to Alfonso de Albuquerque of Portugal.

1513
The Portuguese buy cloves in the Spice Islands.

1579
British explorer Sir Francis Drake visits the Spice Islands on his voyage around the world.

1600
Dutch ships reach the Spice Islands.

1600–64
East India Companies are formed: British (1600), Dutch (1602), Danish (1616), and French (1664).

1605
The Dutch East India Company sets up its first settlement at the Spice Island of Ambon.

1641
The Dutch seize Malacca from the Portuguese.

1667
The Dutch seize control of Aceh on the northern tip of Sumatra and the Spice Island of Tidore.

The process of producing nutmeg and mace.

1 Spice Islanders pick fruits from nutmeg trees.

Trading Companies

Queen Elizabeth I of England (reigned 1558–1603) granted a royal charter to the British East India Company in 1600. It competed with the Portuguese for the spice trade, and was followed two years later by the Dutch East India Company. There was constant conflict between the two companies, but it was the Dutch who succeeded in taking the great trading ports of Southeast Asia. Eventually whole islands came under Dutch control, and by the 18th century the colony was known as the Dutch East Indies (modern Indonesia).

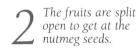

2 The fruits are split open to get at the nutmeg seeds.

Cloves are the dried flower buds of trees from the Spice Islands.

Cinnamon is the inner bark of trees that grew originally in Sri Lanka.

The Spice Islands

The Spice Islands (now called the Moluccas and forming the Maluku province of Indonesia) were the original source of cloves and nutmeg. The islands lie on the equator between the large islands of Borneo and New Guinea. The largest island is Halmahera, but nutmeg originally came from Banda and cloves from Ternate and Tidore.

Black pepper comes from the berries of a vine plant.

SOUTHEAST ASIA

CHINA

INDIA

BAY OF BENGAL

SIAM

PHILIPPINE ISLANDS

PACIFIC OCEAN

COCHIN

SRI LANKA

→ Abreu and Rodrigues 1512
→ Pires 1515–1516

MALACCA

BORNEO

HALMAHERA

JAVA SEA

MOLUCCAS

NEW GUINEA

INDIAN OCEAN

Sailing for Spices

The Portuguese explorer Antonio de Abreu was first to reach the Spice Islands, with his navigator Francisco Rodrigues, in 1512–1513. One of Abreu's officers, Francisco Serrão, was shipwrecked on one of the islands and stayed there for the rest of his life. Tomé Pires was a Portuguese official based in Malacca. They all sailed through the Straits of Malacca and the Java Sea to the Moluccas. The map shows their routes.

Wooden figure of a Dutch East India Company official.

3 *The outer covering of the seed, called mace, is removed and laid out separately to dry.*

4 *Sacks of nutmeg and mace are taken to ships bound for Europe.*

This 15th-century Portuguese illustration shows shipbuilders at work on a caravel.

The Caravel
The original Mediterranean caravel was lateen-rigged, which meant it had triangular sails. It was carvel-built, made of planks fitted edge to edge and nailed onto a frame. It was ideal for coastal voyages, since it could sail in shallow waters. For longer voyages across oceans, caravels were rigged with square sails. This made them faster and easier to handle in stormy weather. Columbus' *Niña* and *Pinta* were caravels (see page 26).

Ship Building
From about 1250, trading ships called cogs were built in the Hanseatic ports of the North Sea. Early caravels were developed by the shipbuilders of the Portuguese prince, Henry the Navigator (see page 23). In 1496, King Henry VII of England (reigned 1485–1509) established a dockyard at Portsmouth, where large cargo vessels were built. In 1513, his son, King Henry VIII (reigned 1509–1547) founded dockyards on the River Thames for building warships.

The Medieval seal of the port of Kiel shows a Hanseatic trading cog.

Triangular lateen sail on the mizzenmast.

Square sail on the mainmast.

The Niña had a square foresail and mainsail. About 65 feet (20 m) long and 20 feet (6 m) across the beam, this caravel had a rounded bow and a square stern with a raised quarterdeck.

Seafaring Vessels

Early voyages were made in small vessels that were easy to sail in coastal waters. They had a large hinged rudder at the stern and adapted well to changing wind conditions and shallow seas. Alterations to the rigging—from triangular to square sails—allowed explorers' ships to become bigger, faster, and suitable for long voyages across uncharted oceans. These vessels could also carry larger crews, though space was still limited and conditions were not easy for the sailors.

Versatile Sails

Triangular sails were first developed by Arab sailors and shipbuilders in the Indian Ocean. Lateen-rigged ships, such as Arab dhows and Portuguese caravels, were nimble and sailed well when the wind came from the side. For long voyages, with the wind behind the ship, square sails filled better and were more effective. This meant that caravels, which could be rigged either way, were versatile vessels.

The carrack had extra topsails and a high stern and forecastle.

The galleon had up to five masts, with a lateen sail at the stern.

New Ship Designs

During the 15th century, the larger carrack (or nao) was developed. Famous examples include Columbus' flagship, the *Santa Maria*, and the most successful of Magellan's ships, *Victoria* (see page 28). The 16th-century galleon was a multi-decked, armed vessel that was developed as a warship but was also useful for trade and exploration. The Dutch fluyt (or flute) was originally designed as a cargo vessel.

The Dutch fluyt had a large cargo bay and tall masts.

Ocean Voyages

By the time of the great age of exploration, sailors had a range of instruments to help them navigate, but they were not always easy to use in heaving seas. This was especially true on long voyages into the uncharted waters that sea captains wanted to explore. Explorers had to remain determined and optimistic, while ordinary seamen were forced to brave difficult, cramped conditions. Maritime exploration was no easy task.

The cross-piece of the sighting staff moved along a sliding scale to give a reading.

An astrolabe helped sailors to navigate using the positions of the stars and planets.

Early Navigation

Navigators had the use of a number of simple instruments to work out their position on the oceans. Several devices were available for determining the ship's latitude, or distance north or south of the equator. An astrolabe was used to measure the angle between the horizon and the sun at noon or the Pole Star at night. The cross-staff (left) was used in a similar way.

A 15th-century illustration of a navigator using an astrolabe at sea.

Aruj was the older of two famous Barbary pirates known as Barbarossa ("Red Beard.")

Piracy

Pirates (also called buccaneers or corsairs) were a common problem, especially for ships carrying valuable cargo. From the 15th century, Muslim pirates attacked ships along the North African Barbary coast of the Mediterranean. Later, English, Dutch, and French pirates robbed Spanish galleons in the Caribbean, while Arab pirates operated off the Indian coast.

Life on Board

On most ships conditions were cramped and overcrowded for the crew. The sailors' diet was made up of salted meat and fish, and hard ship's biscuits, often washed down with beer. Vegetables soon ran out, causing many to suffer from scurvy. Cargo ships were so loaded up that the crew had to sleep on deck, where it was usually wet and uncomfortable.

Keeping Time

Working out longitude (position east or west) was difficult, because that depended on accurate timekeeping. Sailors had ways of working out the ship's speed, such as counting the knots on a rope as it was laid out. They also used hourglasses and various forms of sundials to calculate the passage of time. Experienced navigators used a combination of results to chart a course.

The ship's compass, which has a needle to indicate magnetic north, greatly improved maritime trade by making navigation more accurate.

This portable German sundial dates from 1598. This type of timekeeping instrument was used along with larger devices.

Storms

Stormy seas were a constant threat, and many explorers' ships were sunk and sailors drowned. The Portuguese explorer Bartolomeu Dias (c. 1450–1500) suffered this fate. He was the first to sail around the southern tip of Africa, but storms and an unhappy crew made him turn back after he had passed what he called the Cape of Storms. (It was later named the Cape of Good Hope.) He survived that time, but when he returned in 1500, he drowned off the Cape when his ship was wrecked in a storm.

Bartolomeu Dias fights to save his ship and crew. The storm finally won.

African Exploration

During the 15th century, Portuguese explorers worked their way down the Atlantic coast of Africa. Many of them believed that beyond Cape Bojador lay a tempestuous "sea of darkness," where the devil waited for foolhardy sailors. After this was disproved, great progress was made and trade increased under the guidance of Prince Henry the Navigator. By 1488, Portuguese ships had rounded the Cape of Good Hope and led the way to the Indian Ocean.

This 16th-century ivory mask from Benin, West Africa, is decorated across the top with a row of Portuguese heads.

From the 15th century, these brass weights were used by the Akan people of West Africa to weigh gold for trade with Europeans.

Mansa Musa

One of the richest African empires of the 14th century was that of Mali. From 1312 to 1337, it was ruled by Mansa Musa, who controlled the movement of two important commodities—salt and gold. The Muslim ruler made a famous pilgrimage to Mecca. He was accompanied by a baggage train of at least 80 camels laden with gold, much of which was spent and given away during his stay in Cairo. Musa's journey alerted Europeans to the riches of Africa.

Trade Goods

One of the aims of the Portuguese in exploring the African coast was to establish trading posts. They had a great desire for gold, and soon added ivory and human slaves to their list. The slaves were used to help solve a labor shortage in Portugal. Craftsmen in Benin and elsewhere carved ivory into salt-cellars and other objects that appealed to the Europeans. They traded the objects for guns or cloth.

AFRICA

Exploring the Coast

The map shows the progressive Portuguese exploration of the west coast of Africa, begun by Henry the Navigator. From 1469 to 1474 southward progress was made by Fernão Gomes (active late 15th century), to whom the Portuguese king had granted a trading monopoly. King João II (reigned 1481–1495) continued to promote African exploration and trade, and the southern tip of the continent was finally rounded by Dias (see page 21).

TANGIER · · CEUTA · TUNIS

TUAT · CAIRO

· RIO DE OURO

· ARGUIN

· TIMBUKTU · MECCA

A F R I C A

ELMINA

MOGADISHU

ATLANTIC OCEAN

MALINDI

KILWA

BENGUELA

INDIAN OCEAN

CAPE OF GOOD HOPE

Explorations during Henry the Navigator's time, 1434–1462

Gomes 1469–1474

Explorations under João II, 1482–1488

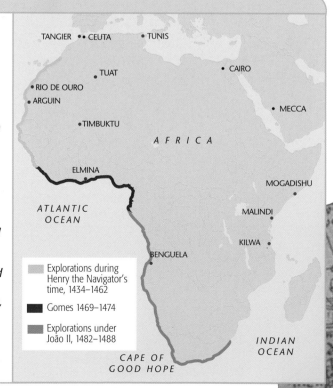

This detail from a 14th-century Catalan atlas shows Mansa Musa receiving a Saharan trader with the offer of a nugget of gold.

AFRICA

1324
Malian ruler Mansa Musa undertakes his spectacular pilgrimage to Mecca.

1415
Portuguese capture the Moroccan port of Ceuta.

c. 1419
Portuguese ships reach the island of Madeira.

1435
Gil Eanes (c. 1395–1445) sails south beyond Cape Bojador ("Bulging Cape").

1441
Africans are taken back to Portugal to be sold as slaves.

c. 1460
Portuguese explorers discover uninhabited Cape Verde islands.

1482
Portuguese build a fort and trading post at Elmina on the Gulf of Guinea (in present-day Ghana).

1486
The kingdom of Benin begins trade with Portugal.

1487–1488
Bartolomeu Dias sails around the Cape of Good Hope.

Below: Portrait of Henry the Navigator taken from an altarpiece painted around 1470. It was commissioned after Henry's death by King Afonso V (reigned 1438–1481) to commemorate progress in Africa.

African Kingdoms

The Portuguese were amazed by the range and power of African cultures. During the 1460s, the Songhai Kingdom took over much of the territory previously covered by Mali. Both kingdoms had become powerful through control of trade across the Sahara. Songhai lost power during the 16th century, as the period of European domination of Africa began, and finally fell to Moroccan invaders in 1591.

Detail of Balthazar, traditionally the African king of the Three Magi, from a painting by Albrecht Dürer of 1504.

Prince Henry the Navigator

Prince Henry (c. 1398–1460) was the fourth son of the Portuguese king João I (reigned 1385–1433). Though known as "the Navigator," Henry rarely went to sea and did no exploring himself. Having organized the fleet that captured the Moorish port of Ceuta, Henry decided to promote Portuguese exploration and expansion in Africa. He brought together a skilled group of mariners, shipbuilders, mapmakers, and astronomers at Sagres, on the Portuguese coast. They formed a successful "school of navigation."

African Slaves

Slavery existed in Africa before the Europeans arrived. Slaves had been a commodity in trans-Saharan trade for centuries. When the Portuguese discovered the uninhabited Cape Verde and São Tomé islands off the African coast, they took slaves there to work the land. Following their colonisation of Brazil in the early 16th century, the Portuguese began transporting them across the Atlantic to work on sugar plantations.

An African bronze sculpture of a Portuguese soldier, from Benin.

A 16th-century illustration of the fort at Elmina, known as the castle of St George.

Slaves were packed into cargo ships so that no space was wasted. Many died on the long journey.

Portuguese Stronghold

In 1482, the Portuguese built a fort at Elmina, on the coast of present-day Ghana. This was intended to protect the gold trade, and the small settlement became a trading post. Before long it was also used as a store for slaves, who were forced to wait in dungeons for slave ships to load them up. The Dutch captured Elmina in 1637, and they continued to use it for the same purpose.

Ivory carving showing the Portuguese capture of slaves.

The Slave Trade

The Portuguese began trading in African slaves in the 15th century. The trade grew in size and importance as Portugal and Spain established colonies in the Americas. They were later joined by Dutch, French, and English slave-traders. Many of the slaves had been captured in warfare by other Africans, who sold them to the Europeans for guns, cloth, and rum. Conditions in holding camps and on long voyages were terrible, and the colonialists simply accepted that large numbers of slaves were lost to disease and death.

Spanish colonists in America used African and Native American slaves to work in mines.

When Ana Nzinga met the Portuguese, she was offered no seat and so called on one of her attendants to crouch.

THE SLAVE TRADE

MOROCCO

EGYPT

to North America and Caribbean

to Arabia

A F R I C A

to North America, Caribbean and Brazil

to India

to Caribbean

to Caribbean and Brazil

ANGOLA

to Mauritius

to Brazil

ATLANTIC OCEAN

to the Americas

INDIAN OCEAN

Across the Atlantic

Many slaves began their horrifying voyage across the Atlantic Ocean at the Guinea coast. The stretch along the shores of present-day Togo, Benin and Nigeria (to the east of the Ivory and Gold Coasts) became known as the Slave Coast. Slaves were taken from as far south as Angola, which was reached by Portuguese explorers in 1483. The so-called Middle Passage transported slaves to the West Indies, where they were sold for sugar and tobacco bound for the European market.

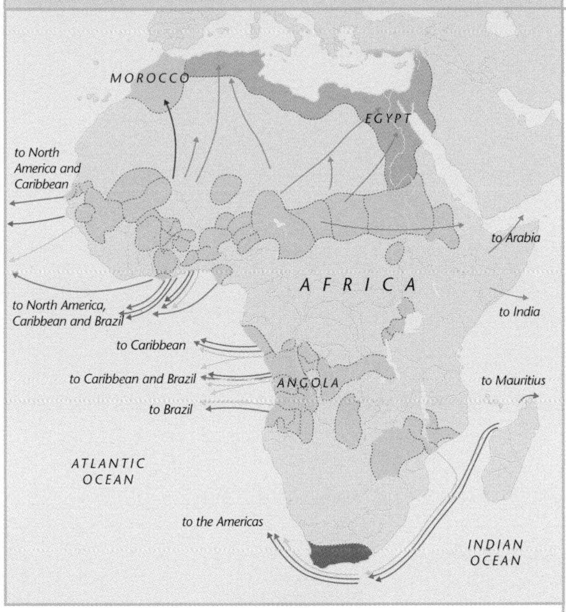

→ Arab routes
→ British routes
→ Danish routes
→ Dutch routes
→ Portuguese routes
→ French routes
→ Moroccan routes

Portuguese possessions
Dutch possessions
Ottoman possessions
African Kingdoms, c. 1750

Queen of Ndongo

Ndongo was the kingdom of the Mbundu people, to the east of Luanda (in present-day Angola). In 1623, Ana Nzinga (c. 1582–1661) met the Portuguese governor in Luanda on behalf of her brother, the ruler of Ndongo. Their lands were a target for slave-traders, and she succeeded in concluding a peace treaty with Portugal. After becoming ruler herself, she converted to Christianity and took the name Ana de Souza. The treaty was later broken by the Portuguese, and the queen helped Africans to rebel against the invaders.

SAILING WEST

NORTH AMERICA

EUROPE

LISBON

ATLANTIC OCEAN

CANARY ISLANDS

SAN SALVADOR

CUBA

HISPANIOLA

AFRICA

CARIBBEAN SEA

SOUTH AMERICA

→ First voyage   → Second voyage   → Third voyage   → Fourth voyage

Columbus' Voyages

Columbus' ships (the Santa Maria, Niña *and* Pinta) *had a total crew of 87. First they sailed to the Canary Islands, where they made repairs and took on supplies, then they sailed west for 33 days, before landing on a small island in the Bahamas. The native islanders called it Guanahani, but Columbus named it San Salvador. Guanahani may have been Watling Island which was officially renamed San Salvador in 1926. Columbus then sailed south to Cuba and Hispaniola.*

Queen Isabella's silver and gold filigree jewelry box. According to legend, the queen pawned jewels to pay for the voyage, but this is untrue.

Royal Patronage

Columbus' plan—his "enterprise of the Indies"—was to reach the Far East by sailing westward. During the 1480s, the Portuguese were trying to do the same thing by sailing around Africa. In 1484, they turned down Columbus' plan, thinking that he miscalculated the voyage. They were right—Columbus underestimated the size of both the Earth and the Atlantic Ocean. In 1492, after the Moors were driven from Granada, King Ferdinand and Queen Isabella of Spain agreed to back his enterprise.

The Voyages of Columbus

Christopher Columbus made some of the most famous voyages in the history of exploration. Yet his plans and expectations were based on miscalculations, and he remained convinced that he had reached the East Indies. In fact, he explored islands which he named the West Indies (they are still called this today) and parts of the coast of Central and South America. Columbus never realized that he had discovered a "New World."

Portrait of Christopher Columbus.

Pages from Columbus' copy of Imago Mundi, *a book of charts and other useful data. Columbus added his own observations and calculations.*

Native American islanders of Guanahani watch Columbus' arrival. The Europeans brought glass beads as gifts, and the islanders offered parrots and cotton thread.

Native Peoples

Believing that he had reached the Indies, Columbus called the islanders he first met—and all the region's native people—"Indians." These people were probably from a group known as Tainos and relatives of the Arawaks. They wore little or no clothing, which Columbus noted in his journal and which probably led Europeans to think of these "Indians" as uncivilized.

Dividing the World

After the first voyage, the Spanish monarchs successfully applied to the pope for control over the lands Columbus had discovered. The Portuguese were unhappy with this, and in 1494 negotiated a treaty with Spain that redrew the line of demarcation. Lands to the west of the line belonged to Spain, those to the east to Portugal. The repositioning later gave the Portuguese their claim to Brazil. The British, Dutch, and French never recognized this division.

The coat-of-arms awarded to Columbus on his return features a design of islands and the anchors of his ships.

BELONGING TO SPAIN

BELONGING TO PORTUGAL

BELONGING TO SPAIN

The demarcation of the world effectively gave the Americas to Spain and the East Indies to Portugal.

COLUMBUS

1451
Columbus is born Cristoforo Colombo in Genoa, Italy, the son of a wool-weaver.

c. 1483
Sails to Elmina on the African Guinea coast.

1492
Sets sail from Palos, Spain (where he is known as Cristóbal Colón), on 2 August; on 12 October lands at San Salvador.

1493
Arrives back at Palos on 15 March.

1493–1496
Second voyage, landing at Puerto Rico, Hispaniola and Jamaica.

1498–1500
Third voyage, reaching Trinidad and the coast of Venezuela.

1502–1504
Fourth voyage, reaching Honduras and the coast of Central America.

1506
Columbus dies in Valladolid, Spain.

Sailing for Spain

Ferdinand Magellan (c. 1480–1521) was convinced that he could reach the Spice Islands by sailing west, past or through the Americas. Having failed to convince the Portuguese king to back him, he turned to Spain. In 1518, he persuaded King Charles I of Spain (reigned 1516–1556) to support his voyage. The following year, he set sail with five ships and about 270 men.

A 16th-century engraving of Magellan sailing through the strait that was later named after him.

Magellan fires a salute as he sets sail from Spain on his famous voyage.

Mutinous Crew

From the outset Magellan had trouble with the Spanish captains of his five ships—the *Concepción*, *San Antonio*, *Santiago*, *Trinidad*, and *Victoria*—and their international crew. One captain was relieved of his command and held prisoner. A later attempted mutiny was put down, another captain was executed, and a third marooned. After sailing into the Pacific and reaching the Philippines, Magellan was killed when he became involved in a fight between rival native groups on the island of Mactan.

Around the World

The first voyage around the world was led by Portuguese explorer Ferdinand Magellan in 1519, but he died during the voyage. Just one of his five ships made it back to Europe after a three-year journey that proved that the Earth is round. Like Columbus, Magellan underestimated the size of the world and its oceans, but he did find a route from the Atlantic to the Pacific. He was followed later in the 16th century by the English seaman Francis Drake.

Sir Francis Drake

Drake was a great English explorer, military commander, and privateer in the service of Queen Elizabeth I. When he sailed from Plymouth in 1577, the crew of his five ships thought they were bound for Egypt, but in fact, Drake planned to sail to the Pacific and plunder unprotected Spanish ports. He not only achieved this, but also became the first Englishman to sail around the world. Elizabeth knighted him on board his ship in 1581.

AROUND THE WORLD

c. 1480
Magellan is born Fernão de Magalhães in northern Portugal.

1519
Magellan sets sail from Sanlúcar de Barrameda, Spain (where he is known as Fernando de Magallanes), on 20 September.

1520
Magellan sails into the Pacific Ocean on 28 November.

1521
Magellan is killed on the island of Mactan (present-day Philippines) on 27 April.

1522
Juan Sebastián del Cano and the Victoria arrive back in Seville, Spain, on 6 September.

c. 1543
Francis Drake is born near Plymouth, England.

1577
Drake sets sail for the Atlantic from Plymouth, on 13 December in the Pelican (later renamed Golden Hind).

1580
Drake arrives back in Plymouth on 26 September.

1596
Drake dies at sea off the coast of Panama.

A 17th-century painting of Sir Francis Drake, flanked by two other Elizabethan sea captains, Thomas Cavendish (left) and John Hawkins (right).

The Land of Giants

In late March 1520, Magellan put to shore at a natural harbor that he named Port St. Julian in what is now southern Argentina. There the Europeans met a group of native Tehuelche people, who were extremely tall and well-built. The newcomers called the land Patagonia, from the Spanish for foot and apparently referring to the locals' large feet.

Magellan and his sailors were amazed at the physical size of the Tehuelches.

CIRCUMNAVIGATION

ASIA

NORTH AMERICA

EUROPE

ATLANTIC OCEAN

AFRICA

INDIAN OCEAN

PACIFIC OCEAN

SOUTH AMERICA

AUSTRALIA

Through the Strait

Both Magellan and Drake sailed through the narrow channel between the southernmost mainland of South America and the islands of Tierra del Fuego. This stormy passage was the shortest and quickest route from the Atlantic to the Pacific Ocean. Magellan then crossed the Pacific to Southeast Asia. Drake headed north, to sack Spanish cities and raid treasure ships.

→ Magellan, 1501–1512   → Magellan, 1519–1521   → Drake, 1577–1580

The Tehuelches hunted the guanaco, a relative of the llama.

A Spanish Empire

In 1520, the same year that Magellan was sailing down the Patagonian coast, Spanish adventurers were overthrowing the Aztec Empire in the Valley of Mexico. Many Aztecs had been reluctant to resist. They believed that the leader of the invaders was their god-king Quetzalcoatl, returning as their legends predicted. Spanish power soon overcame resistance in Central America and, a decade later, in Peru. This was the beginning of a Spanish Empire in the Americas.

The Spaniards' steel weapons gave them a great advantage over the Aztec warriors.

THE SPANISH IN THE NEW WORLD

HAVANA

ATLANTIC OCEAN

TENOCHTITLÁN

BOGOTÁ

PACIFIC OCEAN

SOUTH AMERICA

LIMA • CUZCO

VALPARAÍSO

→ Route of Cortés
→ Route of Pizarro
▪ Spanish territory by 1650

Central and South America

Following the conquest of the Caribbean islands and Aztec lands, Spain created an official colony and appointed a viceroy (or governor) to run it. From 1535, the Viceroyalty of New Spain covered the whole of Central America and the islands of the West Indies. Eight years later, the Spanish added the Viceroyalty of Peru, which included most of the region of the west coast of South America. By this time imperial power stretched from the Valley of Mexico in the north to Valparaíso (in present-day Chile) in the south.

The Conquistadores

The conquistadores (or "conquerors") were more interested in claiming territory for Spain than in exploration. Many were adventurers, seeking fame and fortune. They felt they had the power of Christianity with them, and that the pagan native peoples had no right to their own lands. The conquistadores' journeys and exploits taught Europeans a great deal about the New World that they had discovered.

This 16th-century engraving shows conquistador Vasco Nuñez de Balboa (c. 1475–1519) holding a native chief to ransom.

Hernán Cortés

Hernán Cortés (c. 1485–1547) left Spain for Hispaniola in 1504, and seven years later helped in the conquest of Cuba. In 1518, he led an expedition to the Yucatán Peninsula, where he sank his ships so that none of his men could turn back. On his way inland, Cortés defeated the Tlaxcalans and took some of their warriors into his small army. They headed for Tenochtitlán, capital of the Aztec Empire.

Spanish helmet.

THE SPANISH EMPIRE

1478–1541
Life of Francisco Pizarro.

1485–1547
Life of Hernán Cortés.

1508–1515
Puerto Rico, Cuba, and Jamaica are captured for Spain.

1513
Vasco Nuñez de Balboa crosses Central America to the Pacific Ocean.

1521
Cortés conquers the Aztecs.

1533
Pizarro conquers the Incas.

1535–1549
Rule of Antonio de Mendoza as first viceroy of New Spain.

1543
Establishment of the viceroyalty of Peru.

Aztec weapons, such as this club and spear, were made of wood. The blades were obsidian (volcanic stone).

This plan of Tenochtitlán, from 1524, shows causeways leading to the ceremonial center of the city.

From the Old World

The conquistadores had great advantages in battle, with their powerful weapons—muskets, crossbows, steel swords, and armor. The Aztecs had never seen horses, which gave the Spanish the benefits of speed and height. The Europeans also brought disease with them, especially smallpox, to which the native population had no immunity (see page 34).

The Fall of Tenochtitlán

The Aztec capital was built on islands in a lake. It was connected to surrounding land by causeways. It featured high stepped pyramids and had about 200,000 inhabitants. At first the Aztec emperor, Montezuma II (reigned 1502–1520) welcomed the Spaniards. But there were soon raging battles and, after a three-month siege, Tenochtitlán fell to the invaders.

South America

Francisco Pizarro and other conquistadores were partly motivated to explore South America by their desire for gold. They certainly found plenty of precious metals, most of which they shipped back to Europe. Their desperate wish to find the fabled land of El Dorado further encouraged adventurers to explore the interior of the continent, which they had broadly covered by the end of the 16th century.

A detail of the decorative border of the 1507 map that first named America.

Francisco Pizarro dressed for battle.

This illustrated map of the coast of Brazil dates from 1519.

Naming the New World

In 1507, the German cartographer Martin Waldseemüller (c. 1470–1521) was the first to name the newly discovered continent on a map. He called it America, from the feminine form of the Latin name of a Florentine explorer, Amerigo Vespucci (c. 1454–1512). Vespucci claimed to have sighted the continent in 1499, though his first visit might have been a few years later. He wrote letters describing this *Mundus Novus* (New World), which no doubt came to the attention of the German mapmaker.

Winds and Currents

Toward the end of the 15th century, sailors attempting to reach and round southern Africa realized that they could use the winds and currents of the southern Atlantic better if they sailed further west. In 1500 this tactic took the Portuguese navigator Pedro Alvares Cabral (c.1467–1520) to the coast of Brazil. Cabral claimed the land for Portugal, since it was to the east of the agreed line of demarcation (see page 27).

Atahualpa, last emperor of the Incas, was killed by Spanish conquistadores in 1533.

Pizarro and the Incas

Francisco Pizarro crossed the isthmus of Panama to the Pacific Ocean with Vasco Nuñez de Balboa in 1513. Six years later, he helped found the city of Panama, before making several voyages down the coast of South America. In 1532, he entered the territory of the Inca Empire, later capturing their ruler, Atahualpa. Though he had a small fighting force, Pizarro succeeded in conquering the Incas and plundering their land and treasures. In 1535, he founded Lima, the capital of present-day Peru.

These Spanish doubloons were minted from gold mined in South America.

The Search for Gold

Spanish adventurers went in search of the "golden man," and his legendary wealthy land was soon also known as El Dorado. On their way, the searchers heard further rumors. Some took them to a lake in the highlands of Bogotá, in present-day Colombia, where the Muisca people were thought to be a source of the tales. Lake Guatavita was partially drained by gold-seekers in the 16th century, but without success.

The Legend of El Dorado

Spanish explorers and conquerors heard wondrous tales of treasure in the new continent. They saw Inca gold with their own eyes. One story told of a Native American ruler who had gold dust sprinkled on his skin every day. He would then be rowed out to the middle of a lake and throw gold into the water to please the gods. The Spaniards called this legendary ruler El Dorado (the golden man).

This gold and copper breastplate was made by Muisca craftsmen.

According to legend, the El Dorado ruler went onto the lake by raft. Models of golden rafts have been found in South America.

Pineapple.

New World Plants

Maize originated in Central America and was a staple food of the Aztecs. Columbus took some maize seeds back from Cuba, and by the late 16th-century maize was a well-established crop in southern Europe. Spanish sailors took potatoes from South America for ships' stores, and they soon became a popular food in Europe. Other popular European imports were tobacco, pineapples, cacao beans (for making chocolate), cayenne peppers, kidney beans, and peanuts.

The Europeans took sugar cane to the New World, where it grew very successfully.

Tobacco plant.

Global Movement

The Europeans introduced plants and animals, such as wheat and horses, to America. They also took plants which they knew would grow well there and which they could exploit. Sugar cane and bananas are the best examples. At the same time, they distributed American plants, such as maize, further afield. The Europeans' most unfortunate export was disease, and especially smallpox and measles. These spread rapidly in the New World and wiped out millions of Native Americans.

THE SPREAD OF ANIMALS, PLANTS AND DISEASE

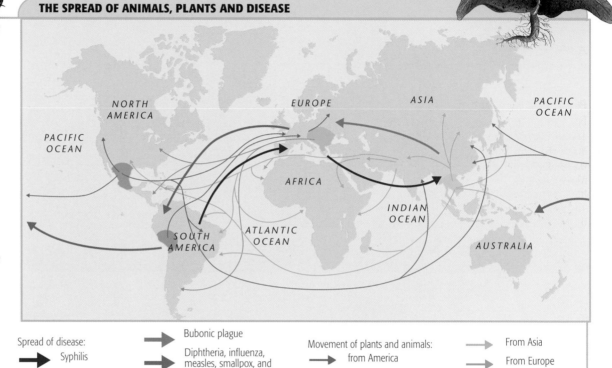

NORTH AMERICA
EUROPE
ASIA
PACIFIC OCEAN
PACIFIC OCEAN
AFRICA
INDIAN OCEAN
SOUTH AMERICA
ATLANTIC OCEAN
AUSTRALIA

Spread of disease:
➤ Syphilis
➤ Bubonic plague
➤ Diphtheria, influenza, measles, smallpox, and whooping cough

Movement of plants and animals:
→ from America
→ From Asia
→ From Europe

New Discoveries

Early explorers found much to interest them in their New World. They took the seeds of many interesting food plants back to Europe. Unfortunately, the newcomers carried European diseases and also brought unwelcome ideas, such as the personal ownership of land and the enslavement of workers. The explorers felt happy about this, since they considered their way of life to be superior to that of native peoples.

Turkeys are native to the Americas. They lived in the wild and were also kept by Native Americans.

Clash of Cultures

Most European explorers and early travelers had little respect for the traditions of native populations. The Europeans considered many native religious rituals to be barbaric. Cortés and his men, for example, were horrified to learn that human war captives were sacrificed at the top of Aztec temple pyramids. The fact that the ritual was intended to provide the gods with blood offerings only made things worse. The Native Americans were seen as "savages."

Figurine of an Inca priest performing a religious ritual.

A Spanish horse and cart. Spanish explorers and colonists introduced both the horse and wheeled vehicles to the Americas. These had a huge impact on the native population.

A 16th-century Aztec illustration of smallpox victims.

Painting and Recording

European explorers usually had an artist on board. The artist's main task was to draw and color maps according to the instructions of the ship's captain or navigator. In 1564, the French painter Jacques Le Moyne de Morgues (c. 1533–1588) began a new tradition by sailing on a colonist ship to Florida. There he painted scenes of Native Americans and their traditional activities.

This engraving of 1591, from an earlier illustration by Jacques Le Moyne de Morgues, shows native people of Florida preparing for a feast.

Missionary Work

The Catholic Church in Europe responded to the great voyages of exploration by sending missionaries to newly discovered territories. During the 16th century, Dominicans, Franciscans, Jesuits, and members of other orders set up missions around the world. They were followed later by Protestant missionaries when the Netherlands and Britain set up trading companies and started overseas colonies. Many Christian missionaries saw it as their task to make sure that native peoples were treated with respect.

In the Americas

The first attempt to convert around 1,500 Native Americans to Christianity was made in the West Indies by Franciscan missionaries. The first diocese was established on Hispaniola in 1511, and then on the American mainland two years later, in Panama. Many friars traveled from place to place to preach, rather than founding missions or churches.

The Italian Jesuit priest Matteo Ricci (c. 1552–1610), dressed in oriental robes, presented navigational and astronomical instruments to the Chinese court.

Jesuits

The order of the Society of Jesus, whose members are known as Jesuits, was founded in 1534. Many Jesuit missionaries sailed with European explorers and colonists to the Americas, Africa and Asia. They believed it was their duty to spread Christian beliefs, and their aim was to set up Roman Catholic missions among pagan populations. Jesuits often wrote detailed reports of local people and their customs, which helped Europeans understand more about the new continents.

This holy-day procession took place in Cuzco, the former capital of the Incas, in around 1660.

This 16th-century lacquer screen shows the arrival in Japan of Francis Xavier (see opposite), along with other missionaries and Portuguese merchants.

Persecution

Many missionaries tried to educate European explorers and improve their attitudes towards native populations. The Spanish Dominican missionary Bartolomé de las Casas (c. 1474–1566) travelled to Hispaniola in 1502. He was determined to improve the lot of local people, and opposed enslavement and persecution by Spanish colonists. In other parts of the world, missionaries were themselves persecuted and expelled.

Bartolomé de las Casas wrote about what he saw, including his famous Report on the Destruction of the Indians.

MISSIONARIES AROUND THE WORLD

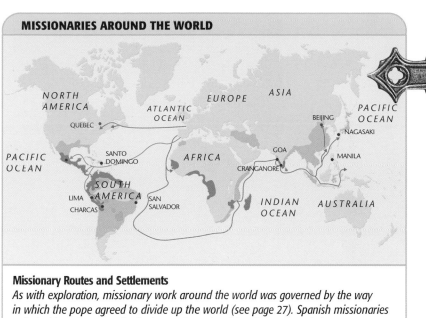

Missionary Routes and Settlements

As with exploration, missionary work around the world was governed by the way in which the pope agreed to divide up the world (see page 27). Spanish missionaries sailed with explorers and colonists to Central and South America. Their Portuguese counterparts concentrated more on Africa and long voyages to the Far East. The Spanish missionaries were generally more successful, and by the early 17th century they were establishing Christian townships in South America.

- ● Centres of major missionary work
- Jesuit areas, 1700
- Main areas of missionary work, 1550
- Other areas of missionary work 1550–c. 1750
- → Portugal
- → Spain
- → France

In Asia

The Spanish Jesuit missionary Francis Xavier (c. 1506–1552) was called the "Apostle of the Indies" by Catholics. He saw it as his great task to convert Asia to Christianity. He first traveled to Portuguese Goa, in India, in 1542. He went on via the Malay peninsula and the Moluccas to Japan, where he arrived in 1549. He sailed on to China, but died before he reached the mainland. Xavier's work was taken up by Matteo Ricci (c. 1552–1610) who founded Jesuit communities and churches in China.

Religions sometimes intermingled. This Christian cross includes an image of the Buddha.

This 17th-century Japanese inro (an ornamental box) is decorated with images of Portuguese men.

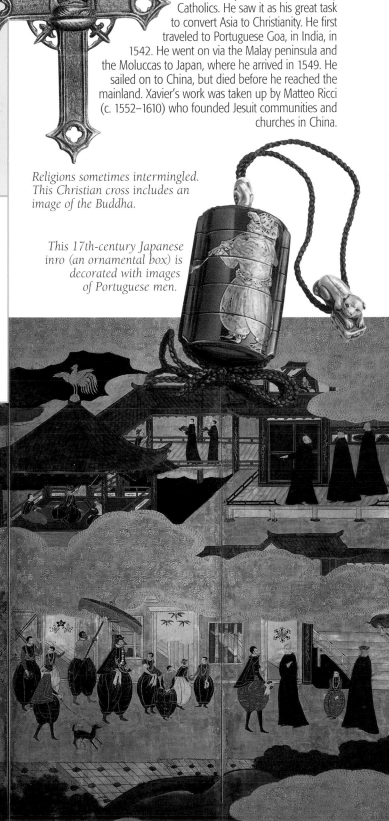

Portrait of John Cabot. King Henry VII of England showed faith in him.

Rediscovering North America

A few years after Columbus' first voyage, other European mariners continued the exploration of North America. To them, this was genuine discovery, though of course the North American continent had been settled many thousands of years earlier by people migrating from Asia. Viking sailors had also voyaged there several hundred years earlier. In the 16th and 17th centuries, pioneering French explorers covered some of the northern territory that was to become Canada. They founded settlements and traded with the Native Americans.

John Cabot

John Cabot (c. 1450–1498) was originally from Genoa, where he was born Giovanni Caboto. He moved to Bristol, in the west of England, and decided after Columbus' voyage of 1492 that he could reach Asia by sailing a more northerly route. He gained permission from King Henry VII and backing from the people of Bristol, and set out with just one ship in 1497. He reached the east coast of North America, but like Columbus thought his "new found land" was Asia. At the same time he discovered the rich fishing grounds near the coast.

Cartier in Canada

The French explorer Jacques Cartier (c. 1491–1557) was sent by King Francis I of France (reigned 1515–1547) to look for gold and a northwest sea passage to the Far East (see page 43). Cartier led three expeditions, and in 1535 sailed up the St. Lawrence River, which he named. He was told by native Hurons that this would lead him to a wealthy kingdom called Saguenay. Cartier explored some of the interior of what is now Canada, but never approached the far northwest.

In the winter of 1535–1536, scurvy broke out among Cartier's men and the local Iroquoians. The Europeans were given a concoction called "annedda," made from white-cedar leaves, and it saved many of their lives.

Exploring the East Coast
The map shows some of the early voyages around the coast. The Corte-Real brothers, from Portugal, used much of Cabot's route. Spanish explorer Juan Ponce de León (c. 1460–1521) sailed further south and became the first to reach Florida. Like many others, Italian navigator Giovanni da Verrazzano (c. 1485–1528) and the Portuguese Estevan Gomez were looking for the Northwest Passage, but they failed to find it.

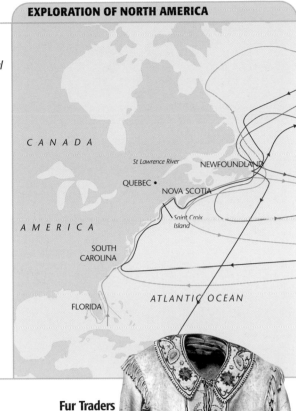

EXPLORATION OF NORTH AMERICA

→ John Cabot, 1497
→ Gaspar Corte Real, 1500
→ Miguel Corte Real, 1501 and 1502
→ Ponce de León, 1513
→ Giovanni da Verrazzano, 1524
→ Estevan Gómez , 1524–1526
→ Lucas Vazquez de Ayllón, 1525
→ John Rut, 1527

Fur Traders
During the 16th century, the French explorers realized the value and potential of animal skins. They traded metal objects and other goods with the Native Americans for furs, and a great demand developed for these in Europe. This encouraged more trappers and traders to voyage across the Atlantic for beaver, fox, marten, and other pelts. Early Quebec became a fur-trading center.

The floral design on this Native American deerskin shirt shows a European influence.

An Iroquois warrior brandishing a club and an axe. Champlain made enemies of the Iroquois people.

Champlain drew this idealised plan of the temporary French settlement on Saint Croix Island (in present-day Maine, US).

Samuel de Champlain
The French explorer and geographer Samuel de Champlain (c. 1570–1635) made his first voyage to North America in 1599. Nine years later he sailed up the St. Lawrence River and founded a fort and French settlement where Cartier had stopped, which was the Iroquoian village of Stadacona. Champlain named it Quebec, and this was the first permanent settlement in the colony that was then known as New France.

Early North American Exploration

Some of the 16th century explorers of North America were looking for mythical places where they thought they could make their fortune. Some say that Ponce de León went to Florida to find the "fountain of youth," a spring that was supposed to restore people's youth and cure sickness. Francisco Vásquez de Coronado (c. 1510–1554) may have been looking for the legendary Seven Cities of Cibola, which were supposed to be filled with gold. But all he and his men found were simple Native American villages.

Native American masks such as this were worn to ward off the evil influence of European newcomers.

Coat of arms of Charles V, King of Spain and Holy Roman Emperor, who authorised De Soto to colonize the southeastern region.

NORTH AMERICA

1513
Ponce de León claims Florida for Spain.

1535
Jacques Cartier sails up the St. Lawrence River.

1540
Francisco Vásquez de Coronado reaches the region of fabled Cibola (in New Mexico).

1541
Hernando de Soto reaches the Mississippi River.

1562
Jean Ribault lands the first French Huguenots in Florida.

1585
Walter Raleigh establishes a first colony at Roanoke Island; the colonists leave with Francis Drake in 1586.

1607
English colonists found the settlement of Jamestown.

1608
Samuel de Champlain founds a French colony at Quebec.

La Florida

The Spanish explorer Ponce de León reached the North American mainland in 1513 and named the region "La Florida." Eight years later, León returned to found a small colony. He was followed by another two Spanish explorers, Panfilo de Narvaez (c. 1470–1528) and Hernando de Soto (c. 1496–1542), who both went ashore in the area of present-day Tampa Bay. They traveled around the Gulf of Mexico (see map opposite).

A 16th-century engraving of Native Americans hunting alligators in Florida.

French Claims

Italian navigator Giovanni da Verrazzano (see page 39) was in the service of France. He sailed along the eastern American coast in 1524. Forty years later, a group of Huguenots (French Protestants) built a fort and set up a colony at the mouth of the St. John's River, near present-day Jacksonville, Florida. This led to the Spanish sending naval captain Pedro Menendez de Aviles (c. 1519–1574) to Florida, where he founded the settlement of St Augustine and defeated the French.

An American chief shows a French explorer the column set up by Jean Ribault (c. 1520–1565) in Florida.

Roanoke

In 1587, more than 100 English settlers landed at Roanoke Island, off the coast of what is now North Carolina. They formed the second colony on the island. Its governor, John White (c. 1540–1618) then sailed back to England to fetch more supplies. Having been delayed by war with Spain, White returned to Roanoke in 1590 but found no sign of the colonists. All that remained was the word "Croatoan" carved on a tree. The Croatoans were Native Americans who lived on a nearby island. No trace was ever found of the settlers.

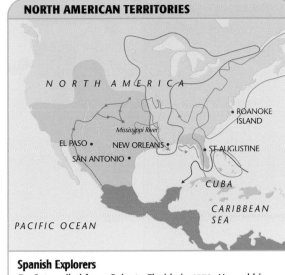

Sir Walter Raleigh (c. 1552–1618), portrayed here with his son, organized the early colonising voyages to Roanoke Island.

John White

John White was probably surveyor-general on Walter Raleigh's voyages of exploration. As an accomplished artist, he drew many scenes of native life in the Americas. His daughter went with him to Roanoke, and she gave birth in 1587 to a baby girl, the first English colonist to be born in America. After the colony disappeared, White never saw his daughter and granddaughter again.

An illustration by John White of a Native American shaman performing a ritual dance.

NORTH AMERICAN TERRITORIES

(map showing North America with EL PASO, NEW ORLEANS, SAN ANTONIO, ST. AUGUSTINE, ROANOKE ISLAND, Mississippi River, CUBA, CARIBBEAN SEA, PACIFIC OCEAN)

Spanish Explorers

De Soto sailed from Cuba to Florida in 1539. He and his men then headed north for what is now Georgia and South Carolina. They then traveled west to the Mississippi, before De Soto died of a fever. At the same time, Francisco Vásquez de Coronado was leading an expedition from the Gulf of California. He reached the prairies of present-day Texas in 1541 and then headed north for Kansas.

→ Route of de León, 1512–1513
→ Route of Coronado, 1539–1543
→ Route of de Soto, 1539–1543
● Spanish trading station

▪ Spanish territory, 1650
▪ Spanish territory, 1750
— French territory, 1750
— British territory, 1750

John White takes leave of his family at Roanoke in 1589.

THE ARCTIC

1553
English explorer Hugh Willoughby (died 1554) reaches Novaya Zemlya in search of the Northeast Passage.

1576
Frobisher sails to Baffin Island in search of the Northwest Passage.

1587
English explorer John Davis (1550–1605) explores the coasts of Greenland and Baffin Island.

1596–1597
Willem Barents and his crew become the first Europeans to survive a winter in the Arctic.

1607–1610
Hudson's first two voyages take him north to Spitsbergen. His third takes him to Hudson Bay.

1631–1632
English explorer Thomas James sails to southern Hudson Bay (into James Bay).

1778
English explorer James Cook (1728–1779) sails through the Bering Strait from the Pacific to the Arctic Ocean.

The Arctic Region

From the 16th century onwards much European exploration was aimed at finding a northern sea route to Asia and the Far East. The English sent many explorers in search of a Northwest Passage across the top of North America. None succeeded, but a great deal was learnt. The journeys also brought the Europeans into contact with the native Inuit people. Dutch explorers concentrated on a possible Northeast Passage, across the top of Siberia. This would eventually be sailed first, but only in 1879.

This English map of the 1500s shows how little was known of the Arctic region beyond Iceland.

Martin Frobisher was one of the most dashing adventurers of his day. Arrested several times for piracy, he was eventually knighted for fighting the Spanish.

Sir Martin Forbisher

The English adventurer and privateer Martin Frobisher (c. 1535–1594) made three attempts to find the Northwest Passage. He took back some "black earth" from the Baffin Island region, which was mistakenly thought to contain gold and caused a great stir. On his third voyage, in 1578, Frobisher sailed with 15 ships and a number of miners, but all they found was "fool's gold."

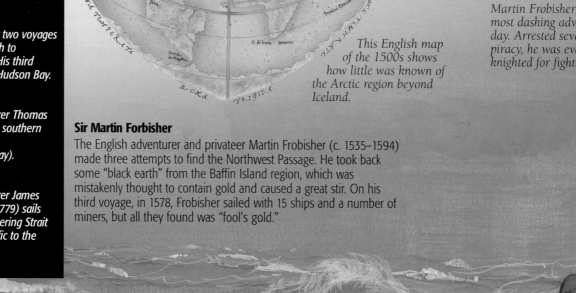

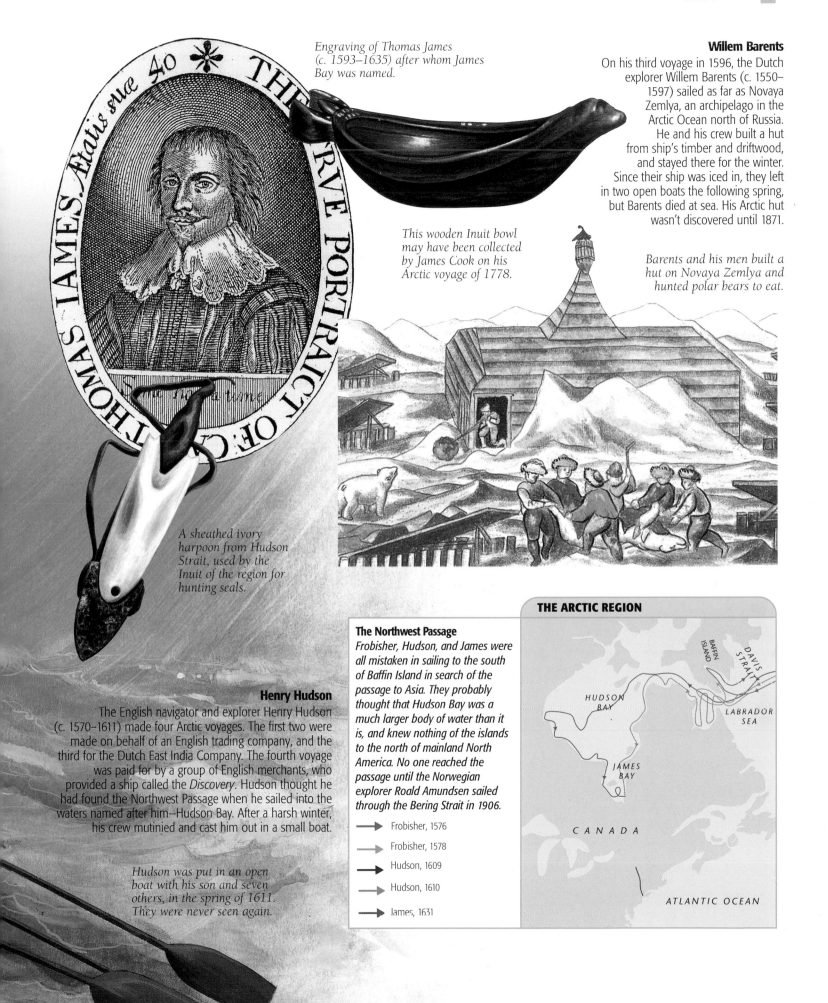

Engraving of Thomas James (c. 1593–1635) after whom James Bay was named.

Willem Barents

On his third voyage in 1596, the Dutch explorer Willem Barents (c. 1550–1597) sailed as far as Novaya Zemlya, an archipelago in the Arctic Ocean north of Russia. He and his crew built a hut from ship's timber and driftwood, and stayed there for the winter. Since their ship was iced in, they left in two open boats the following spring, but Barents died at sea. His Arctic hut wasn't discovered until 1871.

This wooden Inuit bowl may have been collected by James Cook on his Arctic voyage of 1778.

Barents and his men built a hut on Novaya Zemlya and hunted polar bears to eat.

A sheathed ivory harpoon from Hudson Strait, used by the Inuit of the region for hunting seals.

Henry Hudson

The English navigator and explorer Henry Hudson (c. 1570–1611) made four Arctic voyages. The first two were made on behalf of an English trading company, and the third for the Dutch East India Company. The fourth voyage was paid for by a group of English merchants, who provided a ship called the *Discovery*. Hudson thought he had found the Northwest Passage when he sailed into the waters named after him–Hudson Bay. After a harsh winter, his crew mutinied and cast him out in a small boat.

Hudson was put in an open boat with his son and seven others, in the spring of 1611. They were never seen again.

The Northwest Passage

Frobisher, Hudson, and James were all mistaken in sailing to the south of Baffin Island in search of the passage to Asia. They probably thought that Hudson Bay was a much larger body of water than it is, and knew nothing of the islands to the north of mainland North America. No one reached the passage until the Norwegian explorer Roald Amundsen sailed through the Bering Strait in 1906.

→ Frobisher, 1576
→ Frobisher, 1578
→ Hudson, 1609
→ Hudson, 1610
→ James, 1631

THE ARCTIC REGION

BAFFIN ISLAND
DAVIS STRAIT
HUDSON BAY
LABRADOR SEA
JAMES BAY
CANADA
ATLANTIC OCEAN

Australasia and the Pacific

By the 17th century, Dutch, English, and French explorers were discovering many Pacific islands. But they had still not found what they were looking for—a great *Terra Australis* ("southern land"). When they finally got there they found that the smaller islands had been populated thousands of years earlier and that the largest island, Australia, had its own aboriginal population. The greatest Pacific explorer was James Cook, whose discoveries led to European colonization of Australia.

Polynesians

Ancestors of the people of Polynesia (or "many islands") sailed to the region from Southeast Asia around 3,000 years ago. Sea levels were much lower then, and the Polynesians probably used rafts or canoes. The Spanish explorers who sailed from Peru in 1567 searching for a southern Pacific continent, used much larger ships and were amazed to find so many islands with a native population speaking the same language.

The Polynesian island of Moorea was visited by James Cook in 1774.

THE PACIFIC

1568
Spanish explorer Álvaro de Mendaña (1541–1595) reaches the Solomon Islands.

1595
Mendaña discovers the Marquesas Islands (in modern French Polynesia).

1606
Dutch navigator Willem Janszoon (1570–1630) charts part of the coast of Australia.

1642
Tasman reaches the island of Van Diemen's Land (modern Tasmania).

1722
Dutch explorer Jacob Roggeveen (1659–1729) is the first European to see Easter Island.

1767
British captain Samuel Wallis (1720–1795) visits Tahiti.

1768
Bougainville visits the largest of the Solomon Islands (named Bougainville after him).

1770
James Cook claims the east coast of Australia for Britain.

Jean-François La Pérouse

The French explorer Jean-François La Pérouse (c. 1741–1788) left Brest in 1785 for the Pacific. He took a group of scientists on board his two frigates, as well as three illustrators. He visited Easter Island, Hawaii, Samoa, Tonga, and Botany Bay (in New South Wales). From there he sent his journals to Europe on a British ship, before setting sail. He and his crew were never seen again.

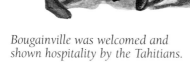

Bougainville was welcomed and shown hospitality by the Tahitians.

Louis-Antoine de Bougainville

The French navigator Louis-Antoine de Bougainville (c. 1729–1811) was commissioned to sail around the world by the French crown. He completed the voyage with two ships from 1766 and 1769. On his way across the Pacific, Bougainville stayed for five months in Tahiti, which he described as an earthly paradise where people lived in happy innocence. He then approached Australia, but did not cross the Great Barrier Reef.

This red honeysuckle was painted in 1773 from a specimen brought back from Australia by Cook.

Cook had use of this chronometer, which allowed him to measure longitude and calculate his position accurately.

THE PACIFIC

ASIA

NORTH AMERICA

ATLANTIC OCEAN

PACIFIC OCEAN

AUSTRALIA

SOUTH AMERICA

SOUTHERN OCEAN

James Cook's Voyages
English captain James Cook made three Pacific voyages between 1768 and 1779. On the first, he sailed to Tahiti, New Zealand, and the east coast of Australia. The second also took him to Easter Island. And on the third voyage he sailed north to Hawaii (which he named the Sandwich Islands), before sailing to the Arctic Ocean (see page 43). On his return to Hawaii, Cook was killed by an islander after a quarrel over the theft of a boat.

→ Cook, 1768–1771   → Cook, 1776–1779

→ Cook, 1772–1775   → La Pérouse , 1785–1788

Officers on La Pérouse's voyage measure and draw the giant stone statues of Easter Island in 1786.

Abel Tasman
The Dutch explorer Abel Tasman (c. 1603–1659) sailed in the service of the Dutch East India Company. He left the island of Java with two ships in 1642 and voyaged to Tasmania, New Zealand, Tonga, and Fiji. He thought Tasmania was part of a larger continent, but sailed around Australia without seeing it. Two years later he returned and sailed into the Gulf of Carpentaria, on the coast of northeast Australia.

Portrait of Tasman with his wife and daughter.

Glossary

Archipelago An expanse of sea scattered with small islands.

Astrolabe An instrument used to show the positions of the planets and stars at any given date or time. The astrolabe was used as a navigational tool by early explorers.

Astrologer A person who studies the influence of the stars and planets on human life.

Astronomer A person who studies the science of the stars and planets.

Bow The forward part of a ship.

Bubonic plague A highly infectious disease characterized by swellings called buboes, found in the armpit or groin. Infection was caused by bites from fleas carried by rats.

Buccaneer A pirate, especially one preying on Spanish settlements in the West Indies during the 17th century.

Caravel A small Spanish or Portuguese ship of the 15th and 16th centuries. It had a broad bow and triangular sails.

Cargo The goods carried by a ship.

Carrack A large square-rigged trading vessel, also sometimes used for warfare.

Cartographer A person who draws and compiles maps and charts.

Chronometer A clock-like instrument designed to calculate longitude at sea, often with great accuracy.

Circumnavigation To travel all the way around the world.

Cog A wide, spacious transport ship of the Middle Ages.

Colony A group of settlers living in a new territory, which may already be occupied by indigenous people.

Compass An instrument that indicates direction, usually with a needle that points to magnetic north.

Corsair A pirate, specifically one operating on the Barbary coast (the Mediterranean coast of North Africa).

Dhow An Arab, lateen-rigged ship.

Diphtheria A contagious disease characterized by difficult breathing, a sore throat, and a fever.

Doubloon A gold coin used in Spain and Spanish America.

Fluyt A Dutch cargo ship from the 17th century.

Fool's Gold A name given to iron pyrites, a mineral that looks like gold but is worthless. It fooled many explorers into believing that they had found gold.

Galleon A heavy, square-rigged ship used between the 15th and 18th centuries. It was a vessel for war or trading.

Hull The main body of a ship.

Indigenous Something that lives naturally in a particular region of the world.

Isthmus A narrow strip of land connecting two larger land areas. For example, Panama before the building of the Panama Canal connected North America with South America.

Ivory The hard, creamy-white-colored material found in elephants' tusks.

Junk A sailing ship from the Far East.

Lateen A rig with a triangular sail.

Latitude The distance of a point from the equator, measured in a North–South direction.

Longitude The distance of a point from the equator, measured in a East–West direction.

Maize A tall cereal originally from Central America.

Measles A disease characterized by fever and red spots.

Mappae mundi A latin phrase meaning "sheet of the world," from which we get the modern English word for map.

Missionary Someone who works to increase membership of the Christian church by converting people from other religions.

Pilgrim A person who makes a journey to a sacred place to show their devotion to God.

Pirate A robber operating at sea.

Portolan maps A 14th-century European navigation chart.

Privateer A privately owned ship that can be commissioned by a government to fight against the enemy in wartime. Also the name for the captain or crew of this kind of ship.

Rigging The ropes used for controlling sails and supporting the mast on board a ship.

Rudder A flat piece attached to the base of a ship, at the stern. It allows it to change course.

Scurvy A disease caused by lack of Vitamin C. Symptoms include spongy gums, loose teeth, and bleeding under the skin. Scurvy used to be common in sailors before it was discovered that consuming limes and other fruit during a voyage prevented the disease.

Slave A person who is treated as the property of another and who is forced to work.

Smallpox An extremely serious and infectious disease. The sufferer develops a fever and pus-filled spots that eventually form scabs.

Stern The rear end of a ship.

Sundial An instrument for telling the time. The sun hits a pointer that casts a shadow onto a cylindrical surface, indicating the hour of the day.

T-O maps Early maps, made by Christian monks, who used a T shape to divide the world into three continents (Europe, Asia, and Africa), surrounded by an O-shaped ocean.

Vellum A strong, cream-colored parchment paper, originally made from calf or pig skin.

Viceroy A governor of a province or colony who rules in place of a king or queen.

Index

Abreu, Antonio de 17
Acre 4, 10, 11
Aceh 16
Africa 4, 8, 10, 14, 15, 22, 26, 29, 32, 34, 36, 37
 – East Africa 4, 5, 11, 12, 13
 – North Africa 20
 – West Africa 5, 22
Akan people 22
Albuquerque, Alfonso de 5, 14, 15, 16
Alexandria 6, 8
Al Idrisi 7, 9, 10, 11
Almeida, Francisco de 15
Americans, Native 34, 35, 33, 38, 39, 40, 41
Angola 25
Arabia 7, 14
Arabian Sea 5, 10, 12, 13
Arabs 17, 19
Arawaks 27
Arctic 4, 5, 42, 43, 45
Arctic Ocean 5, 42, 45
Argentina 29
Armundsen, Roald 43
Aruj (Barbarossa) 20
Asia 4, 10, 11, 13, 34, 36, 37, 38, 43, 45
 – Central Asia 6
 – Far East 26
 – Southeast Asia 4, 7, 14, 16, 29, 44
astrolabe 20
Atahualpa 32
Atlantic Ocean 7, 15, 22, 24, 25, 26, 29, 30, 32, 34, 39
Australasia 4, 44, 45
Australia 5, 29, 34, 37, 44, 45
Aztecs 5, 30, 31, 34, 35

Babylonians 8
Baffin Island 4, 5, 7, 42, 43
Bahamas 26
Balboa, Vasco Nuñez de 30, 31, 32
Balthazar 23
Banda 17
Barbarossa (Aruj) 20
Barbary Coast 20
Barents, Willem 5, 42, 43
Battuta, Ibn 4, 5, 10, 11
 – Rihlah (Travels)
Beijing 37
Benin 22, 23, 24, 25
Bering Strait 5, 42, 43
Bogotá 30, 33
Borneo 17
Botany Bay 44

Bougainville, Louis-Antoine de 5, 44
Brazil 24, 27, 32
bubonic plague 34
buccaneers 20
Buddhists 7

Cabot, John (Caboto, Giovanni) 38, 39
Cabral, Pedro Álvares 32
cacao beans 34
Cairo 22
Calicut 10, 13, 14, 15
camels 6, 7, 11
Canada 38, 39
Canary Islands 26
Cape Bojador 22, 23
Cape of Good Hope 15, 21, 23
Cape of Storms 21
Cape Verde Islands 23, 24
caravels 18, 19, 26
Caribbean 20, 30
carracks 14, 19, 26
Cartier, Jacques 5, 39
Casas, Bartolomé de las 36
 – Report on the Destruction of the Indians 36
Cathay see China
Cavendish, Thomas 28
cayenne pepper 34
Central America 4, 26, 27, 30, 31, 34, 37
Ceuta 23
Ceylon (Sri Lanka) 5, 12, 17
Champlain, Samuel de 39, 40
Chang-an 7
Chang Jiang River 13
Charles I, King of Spain 28, 40
Chile 30
China 4, 6, 8, 9, 10, 11, 12, 37
 – Great Wall of 9
Chittagong 13
Cholula 5
chronometer 44
Chuan-chou 10
Church, Roman Catholic 14, 36, 37
Cibola, Seven Cities of 40
cinnamon 17
cloves 16, 17
Cochin 14, 15
cogs 18
Colombia 33
Columbus, Christopher 5, 12, 18, 19, 26, 27, 28, 34, 38
 – Niña 18, 26
 – Pinta 18, 26
 – Santa Maria 19, 26
Conquistadors 5, 30, 31, 32

Constantinople 10
Cook, James 5, 42, 43, 44, 45
Corte-Real, Gaspar 39
Corte-Real, Miguel 39
Cortés, Hernán 5, 30, 31, 34
corsairs 20
Croatoans 41
Cuba 26, 31, 34, 41
Cuzco 30, 36

Da Gama, Vasco 12, 14, 15
Davis, John 42
De Covilhão, Pero 14, 15
Del Cano, Juan Sebastian 28
Delhi 10
deserts 6
De Souza, Ana (see Nzinga, Ana)
dhows 10, 19
Dias, Bartolomeu 21, 22, 23
diphtheria 34
Don River 8
doubloons 33
Drake, Sir Francis 5, 16, 28, 29, 40
 – Golden Hind (formerly Pelican) 28
Dürer, Albrecht 23

Eanes, Gil 23
Easter Island 5, 44, 45
East India Companies
 – British 16
 – Dutch 16, 17, 43, 45
East Indies 26
Egyptians 6, 8
El Dorado 32, 33
El Paso 41
Elizabeth I, Queen of England 16, 28
Elmina 23, 24, 27
 – Castle of St George 24
Eratosthenes 8
Ericsson, Leif 4, 7
Eric the Red 7
Europe 8, 15, 17, 26, 28, 29, 32, 34, 36, 37, 39

Fa Hsien 7
Faeroe Islands 7
Ferdinand, Spanish king 26
Fiji 45
Florida 5, 35, 39, 40, 41
fluyt 19
fool's gold 42
Francis I, King of France 39
Frobisher, Martin 5, 42, 43

galleons 19, 20
Genoa 27

Ghana 23, 24
Goa 4, 14, 15, 37
gold 22, 23, 24, 32, 33
Gold Coast 25
Gomes, Fernão 22
Gómez, Estevan 39
Great Barrier Reef 44
Greeks, ancient 6
Greenland 4, 7, 42
guanacos 29
Guanahani 26, 27
Gulf of California 41
Gulf of Carpentaria 45
Gulf of Guinea 23

Halmahera 17
Hanseatic Ports 18
Hawaii 44, 45
Hawkins, John 28
Henry VII, King of England 18, 38
Henry VIII, King of England 18
Henry the Navigator 18, 22, 23
Hispaniola 26, 27, 30, 36
Homem, Diego 5
Honduras 27
Hormuz 4, 10, 11, 12, 13
horses 34
Hsüan-Tsang 4, 5, 7
Hudson Bay 5, 42, 43
Hudson, Henry 5, 42, 43
 – Discovery 43
Hudson Strait 43
Huguenots 40
Hurons 39

Iceland 7
Imago Mundi 26
Incas 5, 31, 32, 33, 36
India 4, 5, 7, 12, 14, 15
Indian Ocean 7, 10, 11, 12, 15, 19, 22, 29, 34, 37
Indonesia 17
Inuits 42, 43
Iroquoians 39
Isabella, Spanish queen 26
ivory 22, 24
Ivory Coast 25

Jacksonville 40
Jamaica 27, 31
James Bay 42, 43
James, Thomas 42, 43
Jamestown 40
Janszoon, Willem 44
Japan 5, 37
Java 45

Java Sea 17
Jerusalem 8
Jesuits 5, 36, 37
João ll, King of Portugal 22

Kansas 41
Karakorum 10
Kenya 12
Khan, Kublai 10, 11
Khan, Mongke 10
Kiel 18

Lake Guatavita 33
La Pérouse, Jean-François 44, 45
Le Moyne de Morgues, Jacques, 44
Lima 32, 34
Lisbon 15, 16

mace 16, 17
Mactan Island 5, 28
Madeira 23
Magellan, Ferdinand 5, 19, 28, 29, 30
– *Concepciòn* 28
– *San Antonio* 28
– *Santiago* 28
– *Trinidad* 28
– *Victoria* 19, 28
maize 34
Malacca 5, 13, 16, 17
Malacca Straits 13, 17
Malay peninsula 37
Mali 5, 22, 23
Malindi 13, 15, 22
Maluku province 17
mappae mundi 9
Marquesas Islands 44
Marshall Islands 8
Mbundu people 25
measles 34
Mecca 4, 10, 11, 12, 13, 22, 23
Mediterranean Sea 7, 8, 14, 18, 20
Mendaña, Alvaro de 5
Mendoza, Antonio de 31
Menendez de Aviles, Pedro 40
Mexico 4, 30
Middle Passage 25
Ming Period 12
Mississippi River 41
Mogadishu 15, 22
Moluccas (Spice Islands) 5, 16, 17, 28, 37
Mongols 6, 10, 12
Montezuma l, King of the Aztecs 31
Muisca people 33
Musa, Mansa 22, 23

Nanjing 13
Narvaez, Panfilo de 40
New World 5, 26, 30, 32, 34
Newfoundland 38, 39
New France 39
New Guinea 17
New Orleans 41
New Zealand 4, 7, 45
Nigeria 25
Nile River 8
North America 4, 7, 29, 34, 37, 38, 39, 40, 41, 42, 43, 45
North Carolina 41
Northeast Passage 42
North Sea 18
Northwest Passage 5, 39, 42, 43
Norway 7
Novaya Zemlya 42, 43
nutmeg 16, 17
Nzinga, Ana (Ana de Souza) 24, 25

Pacific Ocean 4, 5, 7, 8, 28, 29, 30, 31, 32, 34, 37, 44, 45
Palos 27
Panama 5, 28, 32, 36
– Isthmus of 32
Patagonia 29, 30
Persia 6
Persian Gulf 12
Peru 30, 31, 32, 44
Philippines 11, 28
Phoenicians 6
pirates 20
Pires, Tomé 17
Pizarro, Francisco 5, 30, 31, 32
Polynesians 4, 7, 44
Polo, Marco 4, 10, 11
Polo, Niccolò, 10
Ponce de León, Juan 5, 39, 40, 41
Port St Julian 29
portolan maps 8
Portsmouth 18
Portugal 5, 22, 24, 25, 27, 28, 32, 37, 39
Ptolemy 8
– *Guide to Geography* 8
Puerto Rico 27, 31

Quebec 39, 40
Quetzalcoatl 30

Raleigh, Sir Walter 5, 41
Red Sea 12
Ribault, Jean 40
Ricci, Matteo 5, 36, 37
Rio de Ouro 22

Roanoake Island 5, 40, 41
Rodrigues, Francisco 17
Roggeveen, Jacob 5, 44
Roger ll, King of Sicily 9, 10
Romans, ancient 6
Rubruck, William of 10
Russia 43
Rut, John 39

Sagres 23
Saguenay 39
Sahara 23
St Augustine 40, 41
Saint Croix Island 39
St. John's River 40
St. Lawrence River 5, 39
Samoa 7, 44
Sandwich Islands 45
Sanlucar de Barrameda 28
San Salvador 26, 27, 37
Sanskrit 7
São Tomé Islands 24
Scottish Islands 7
scurvy 20, 39
Seville 28
Serrão, Francisco, 17
Siberia 42
Sicily 10
Silk Road 6
slaves 22, 23, 24, 25
Slave Coast 25
smallpox 31, 34, 35
Solomon Islands 5, 44
Somalia 12
Songhai Kingdom 23
Soto, Hernando de 40, 41
South America 4, 26, 29, 30, 32, 33, 34, 37
South Carolina 41
Southern Ocean 45
Spain 5, 24, 27, 28, 30, 31, 37, 40
Spice Islands (Moluccas) 5, 16, 17, 28, 37
spices 6, 16
Spitsbergen 42
Stadacona 39
Sri Lanka (Ceylon) 5, 12, 17
sugar 25, 34
Sumatra 5, 7, 12, 16
sundials 20
Surabaya 13
Suzhou 13
Swahili 12
syphilis 34

Tahiti 44, 45

Tainos 27
Tang Empire 7
Tangier 10, 11, 22
Tasman, Abel 5, 44, 45
Tasmania 5, 45
Tehuelche indians 29
Tenochtitlán 30, 31
Ternate 17
Terra Australis 44
Thames, River 18
Tidore 16, 17
Tierra del Fuego 29
Timbuktu 22
Tlaxcalans 31
Tobacco 25, 34
T-O Maps 8, 9
Togo 25, 45
Tonga 7, 44, 45
"treasure ships" 12
Trinidad 27

Valladolid 27
Valparaíso 30
Van Diemen's Land *see* Tasmania
Vázquez de Ayllón, Lucas 39
Vásquez de Coronado, Francisco 40, 41
Venice 9, 10, 11
Vespucci, Amerigo 32
Vikings 7, 38
Venezuela 27
Verrazzano, Giovanni de 39, 40

Waldseemüller, Martin 32
Wallis, Samuel 44
Watling Island 26
West Indies 25, 26, 30
wheat 34
White, John 41
whooping cough 34
Willoughby, Hugh 42

Xavier, Francis 5, 36, 37
Xi Yang (the Indian Ocean) 13

Yuan Dynasty 10, 11
Yucatán Peninsula 31
Yunna 12

Zamorin 15
Zheng He 5, 12, 13
Zhu De 12